SPORTSCENTER POEMS

Poems by
Christoph Paul

Art by
Jim Agpalza

Copyright © 2018 by Christoph Paul, Jim Agpalza

Cover and art by Jim Agpalza

David Beckham guest art by Spider B.

ISBN:

CLASH Books

PO BOX 487 Claremont, NH 03743

All rights reserved.

This book is a work of comic art, parody, & poetry. Names, characters, businesses, places, incidents and events are either the products of the author's imagination or used in a fictitious manner. Any resemblance to actual persons, living or dead, or actual events is purely coincidental.

No part of this book may be reproduced in any form or by any electronic or mechanical means, including information storage and retrieval systems, without written permission from the author, except for the use of brief quotations in a book review.

Acknowledgements

Christoph Paul

I have to thank the guy, monkey, or neanderthal who invented balls—you have saved me from having existential crisis. My bro Brad for telling poems are ok but they are better with pictures, my dad for introducing me to horror and heartache of being a South Florida sports fan (come back Lebron!), the 2018 National Champions UCF Knights, and my wife for forgiving me every time I tune her out when I'm watching football, basketball, soccer, and baseball when it is the playoffs. Sorry, I don't like hockey, there will be no hockey poems because it's lacrosse on Ice.

Jim Agpalza

I would like to thank my wife and kids for being so patient with me. I'd also like to thank Robert Crumb and Ralph Steadman for inspiring line work. And to all the sports fans out there who may or may not like me by the end of the book, thank you, bro. It was a good run, huh?

"Lennox is a conqueror? No. I'm Alexander. He's no Alexander. I'm the best ever. There's never been anybody as ruthless. I'm Sonny Liston. I'm Jack Dempsey. There's no one like me. I'm from their cloth. No one can match me. My style is impetuous. My defense is impregnable. And I'm just ferocious. I want your heart. I want to eat his children. Praise be to Allah."

- **Mike Tyson**

Lance Armstrong

I lost my other ball
When I dated Sheryl Crow.
But I never cheated on her.
If it makes you happy,
People still call me awful names
But no one is as mean as cancer—
Not even the French.
My legacy is ruined,
And that song by Sheryl Crow
Everyday is a Winding Road,
Is not about me, none of her songs are,
But I'm the only famous bicyclist,
So suck my ball, I'm going for a bike ride.

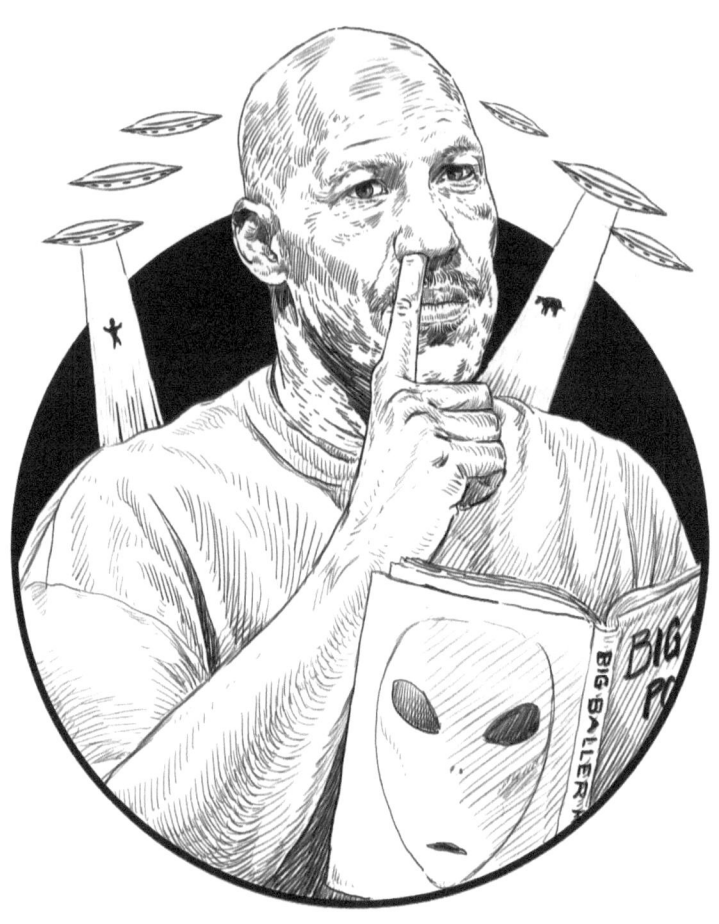

Lavar Ball

Big Baller Poetry books are coming soon!

I am going to write some haikus with my
Boogers
And it's gonna be $399.95 book.

Gonna collab with that Milk & Honey girl,
Get paid in champagne,
And drink Bloody Marys
Made out of David Stern's blood.

My boys gonna rub
their sweaty balls
all over the page
until they invent their own language.

Then we gonna sell this book to aliens
And they gonna pay us in spaceships—
I ain't gonna let Trump ride with us.

Big Baller Spaceships was always the plan.
I've seen Space Jam, and the Ball Family
Is going to be the only Ballers on Mars.

David Beckham

I made Fauxhawks cool
But I could not save soccer
In America

Odell Beckham Jr.

I got such good hands
That in the future
They're gonna clone me
And splice me
With Ant-Man's powers
And have me livin'
Deep in vaginas—
Catching all the sperms.
Odell clones are gonna put
Condoms, the pill,
And the diaphragm
Out of business.
Giants baby!

Bill Belichick

When I first prayed
To Satan
he couldn't hear me
Because even Lucifer
wouldn't go to Cleveland
But the dark Lord
followed me
to New England
and I gave my soul
for a sixth round pick

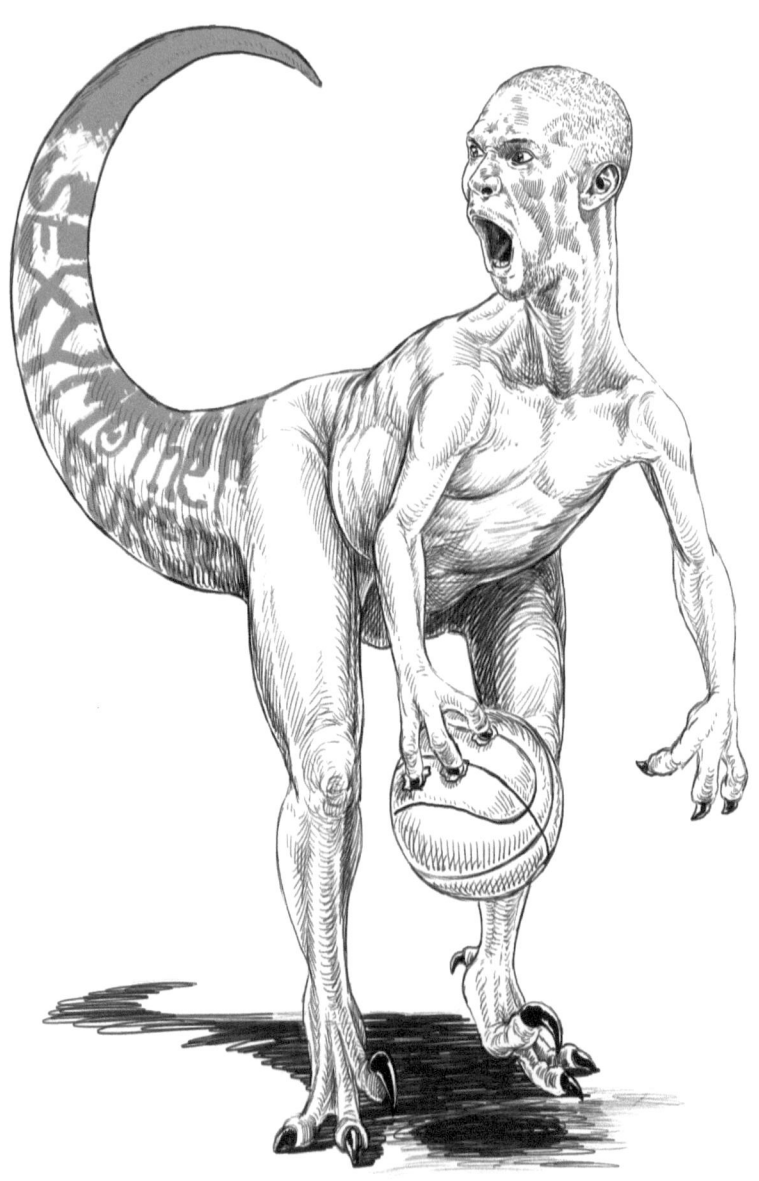

Chris Bosh

Lebron and me stopped being friends
After we watched Jurassic World.
We were having so much fun
And that Chris Pratt sure is funny,
But when Blue & the raptors got on screen
I popped a big boner in my AND1 Shorts.
Lebron shook his head & left,
But I starred right at the screen,
As those raptors ran through the fields
Looking like sexy ass bosses.
Watching that movie inspired me
To become a writer.
So I've been writing kindle erotica
About sexy raptors.
Everything is sexier, with raptors;
That 50 shades movie was boring,
But it would have been dope
If Mr. Grey was a raptor.
So now I'm hooking up
With raptor-romance writer
Chuck Tingle, to show that love is real.

Tom Brady

Did you know that my Super Bowl rings cannot
Be magnetized by Magneto—theoretically.

The D12 method can make you a god.

Some people are just born special, like my wife.
Giselle's vagina caries so much power & magick
That the Earth could stop spinning
When she hits menopause.

But for the rest of us, we need to study
Pliability, And eat our avocados to become
Angels among men.

But it doesn't stop there, my trainer,
Alex G. is teaching me to defy death.

He is a brujo with ancient wisdom
Of the Mayans and secrets of the Great Spirit.

And for $17.76 you buy my book
On Amazon & you can live forever
Achieving a lifetime of peak performance.

Ryan Braun

I really didn't use performance enhancers.

What really are performance enhancers?

No one knows,
some it call it steroids,
but what really is a steroid?

Sounds like a car stereo to me.

I listen to music, that gets me pumped up,
that gets me swinging better,

so if I play music on a stereo
& if that is a stereo-oid then yeah...

I use performance enhancers.

Dez Bryant

Definitions & history of a catch...

Bing Search: intercept and hold (something that has been thrown, propelled, or dropped). Middle English (also in the sense 'chase.')

History: from Anglo-Norman French and Old Northern French cachier, variant of Old French chacier, based on Latin captare 'try to catch,' from capere 'take.'

Dictionary.com: capture (a person or animal that tries or would try to escape.)

Encyclopedia.com: reach in time and board (a train, bus, or aircraft.)

Google: Verb—intercept and hold (something that has been thrown, propelled, or dropped). Noun— an act of catching something, typically a ball.

Urban Dictionary: 1) an attractive person who you feel...

2) The abbreviation for the term *catchya* which is an Australian term which means catch you later or goodbye...

3) To be on the receiving end of a lap dance or twerk session...

NFL: ¯_(ツ)_/¯

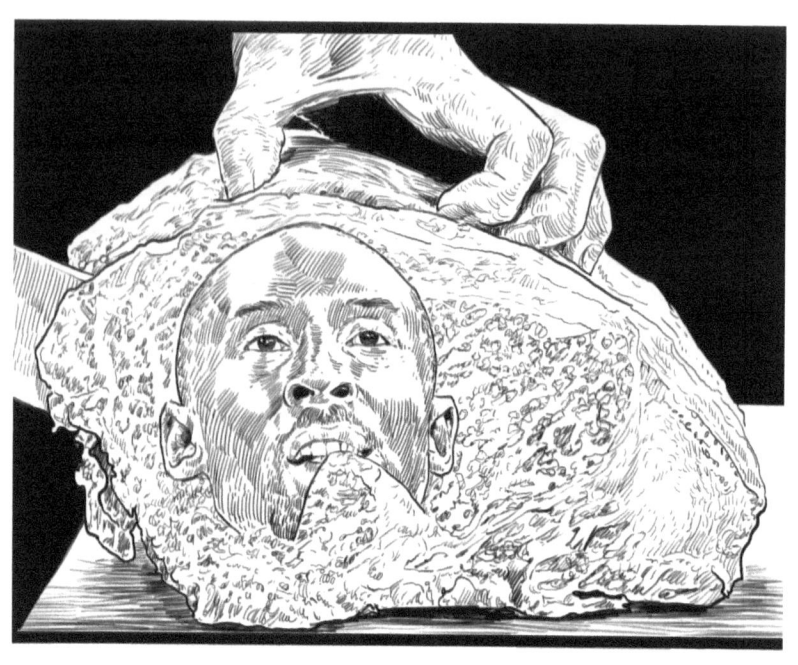

Kobe Bryant

I'm the Mamba,
I strangle trophies
but I don't choke,

except for that girl up in Colorado.

But on the basketball court
I take it the hole
with smoothness.

I'm a champion, I ain't got time for
big men who are soft like marshmallows.

Those motherfuckers end up roasted
by the heat I bring on the court.

I need champions,
killers, well, metaphorically
cause you can't be in jail
and win a championship.

But now, the game is done, but I still
compete and I am still a winner.

I have starring contests with my Oscar,
and I win every time.

Mamba Out.

Reggie Bush

I fucked a Kardashian
Won a Super Bowl
And I peaked in college—
I'm the American Dream, bitch.

Pete Carrol

I'm so pumped up right now, bro!!!
Competition!!! This poem better
be the best it can be!!! It better
have heart, have soul— it doesn't
need to stand tall. Look at Russell
Wilson & get woke!!! It just needs
to be better than those hippy poets
in San Francisco!!!!!!! if you can beat
those beat & slam poets in San Fran
then you are true poet champion!!!!!

Carmelo

I tried to open up my own club in Oklahoma
but it ended getting turned into a farm.

I told my crew I needed solid beats
and lots of hoes,
but these muthafuckas brought me
back gardening tools,
and those vegetables
that makes your shit red.

But I rolled with it and started farming,
now I have 6th biggest farm in the county.

After practice I go get crunk in my cornfields,
thinking of New York City, where hoes are hoes
and the garden wasn't my backyard.

Colin Cowherd

Look guys,
I just don't like Christoph Paul.
I don't like his poems.
What's the deal here?
Who is even the market?
Guys that like spots?
Nope. They don't read.
They listen, they watch, but they don't read.
Reading is basically what women do,
maybe homosexuals, I don't' know.
I love the gays, I do, but none of them
love my show. They listen to NPR and read
poetry, but do people want their NPR and their
sports radio mixed together? I don't think so.
I think this book is dumb. This is a dumb book
idea & Christoph Paul is pretty dumb.
And don't get me started on the artist,
Jim Agpalza—he is a dick who draws dicks.
The Herd won't read this. Will they?

Mark Cuban

One-day sharks will replace all athletes.
Billionaires know this truth.
This is why me and Trump fear sharks so much.

To survive, we will all face the Shark Tank,
But the sharks with walk on land
With their Elon Musk Protons packs.

I've seen Deep Blue Sea 87 times,
Cause it lays out the prophecy.

△ are putting secret messages
In all the shitty shark movies
About the singularity shark future.

That's why I guest-starred
In Sharknado 3 as the president—
△ made me be in the film.

For humanity to survive,
We will have to evolve
Into Godzilla sized cats.

The Singularity Sharks Humaniod Cat War of 2200
Will be the defining moment of humanity!

We must dive into the shark tanks
And defeat them!

Then you, me, and Mr. Wonderful
Will eat cheese and drink wine
After we are victorious!

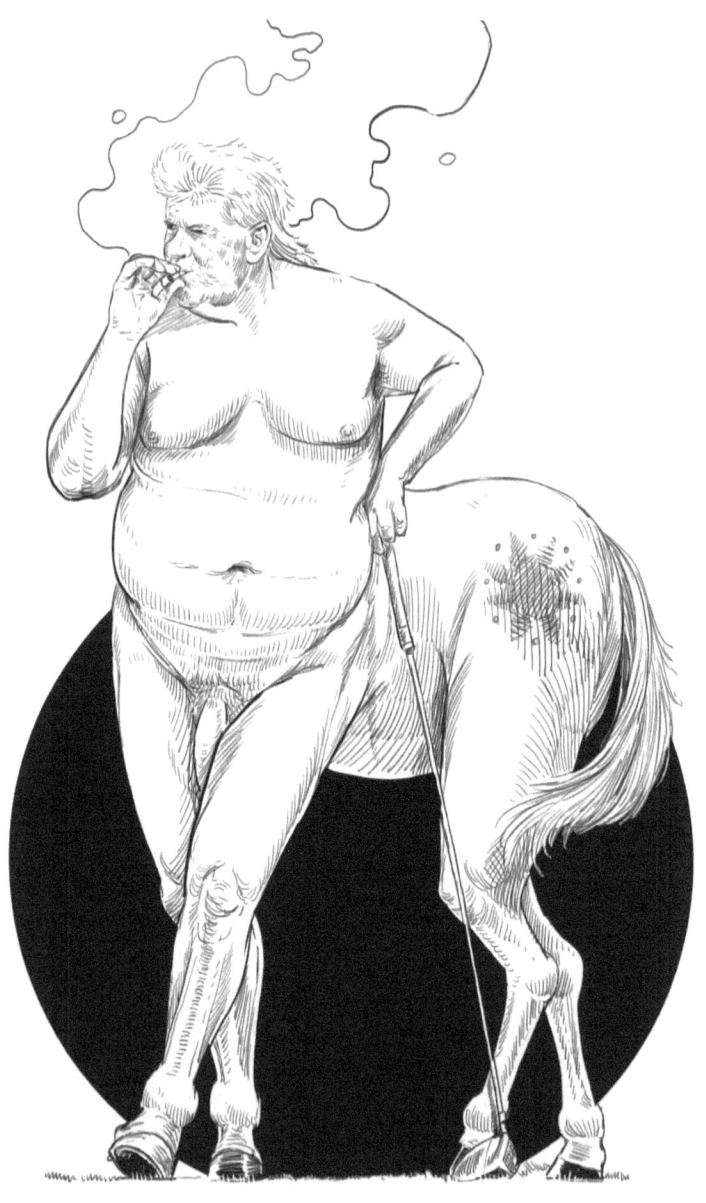

John Daly

Golf is only fun
When you're drunk as fuck, screaming,
"Fore!" while dropping ludes.

R.A. Dickey

I like to think of the
knuckle ball

as a kind hearted man
with a small penis

He ain't going to wow you
or throw magic down the middle

But he's got magic
in his fingers

He's got magic
in his heart

Duke Blue Devils

Featuring G. Allen

When you look like Ted Cruz
And have a .429% shooting percentage
The world will hate you.

Duke is best college basketball team
Because it is funded by the Illuminati.

Coach K is a high member
Of the Morning Stars
And he has taught me
I am a Light Bringer.

At night we sacrifice
North Carolina chickens
And recite Luciferian chants
To increase my wingspan.

That is why
White basketball players
Excel here,

We are blessed
With Illuminati moon magic powered
By Blue Devils.

Kevin Durant

Listen y'all.
This is important.
There is an alien race of mites
Living on my head!
Space Jam was a message
To the alien mites
To live in the hair of the next Jordan.
So I haven't brushed my hair
In 87 months!
The alien! They won't let me
Brush my damn hair,
And NBA Championship trophies
Is what they eat to survive—
That is why I left Oklahoma
And don't brush my hair—
Because I got aliens
Living in my hair, man!

Herman Edwards

(coaching a soccer team)

YOU
PLAY
TO
TIE
THE
GAME
HELLO!?!?

Brett Farve

I like to think of sending out dick pics
Like running the west coast offense.
It's finesse, and about angles,
Turning a few inches
Into a touchdown.
It ain't about dropping bombs
It's about the element of surprise
It's about knowing if your wide receiver
Is open, and if not, you still sling it in there.

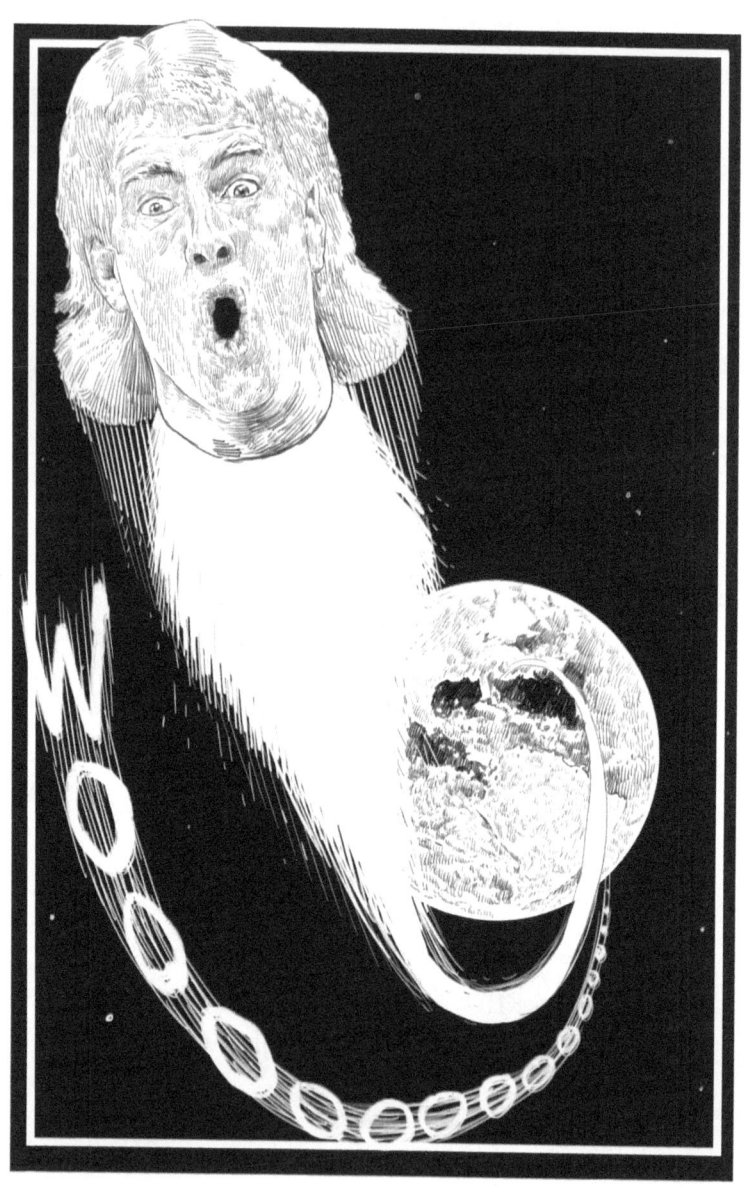

Ric Flair

WoooOooooOh
It's the call of Dionysus
WoooOooooOh
It's wide-open vaginas
WoooOooooOh
The vibration of balls & ovaries
WoooOooooOh
I conquer nature, boy, & emjois
WoooOooooOh
Is what the Gold on my belt sings
WoooOooooOh
Even hobbits know,
I'm the one true king
WoooOooooOhoooOoooOhoooOoooOh

George Foreman

I used to punch faces
And make them bloody
Like the steaks
You can cook on my grill.
My momma said I was ugly
And so did the neighborhood kids.
But I cooked my feelings on the grill,
And they gave me muscles so I could feed
Fools knuckle sandwiches.
But let me tell you something,
If I ever see that Pedo, Jared from Subway,
He gonna taste my right hook,
So don't you go and support
Those Pedo Sandwiches.
Instead, go buy yourself
A George Foreman grill!

Ozzie Guillén

Fuck you
Fuck poetry
Go fuck yourself,
Tu fucking Pendejo

Blake Griffin

Some people say I'm soft.

I asked Malcolm Gladwell,
to write one of his essays
to prove everyone wrong

Redheaded brothers got to
stick together, you know.

His study concluded that moving to Detroit
would deduct my softness by 36.7%.

I like here it in Detroit
I'm getting hard
Hanging out with clown wrestlers
drinking Faygo.

After practice, I hang with Juggalos
and we throw bottles at school busses.

The weather is terrible but the clown make up
keeps me warm and the smog air gets me high.

I'm hard as fuck living that Juggalo Life.

Gronk

Me like football
Me like boobies
Me like fist pump
Me like boobies and fist pump music
Me like 69
Me not like math
Me like playbook, good book
Me no like no other books
Me like dogs and kitty cats
Me no like Eagles
Me no like Giants
Me like movie Facing The Giants
Me no like Giantess Porn
Me like Dwarves.
Me like Tom Tom
Me no like his food
Me like Jersey Shore
Me like Bill Bill
Me no like football Bills
But me love football

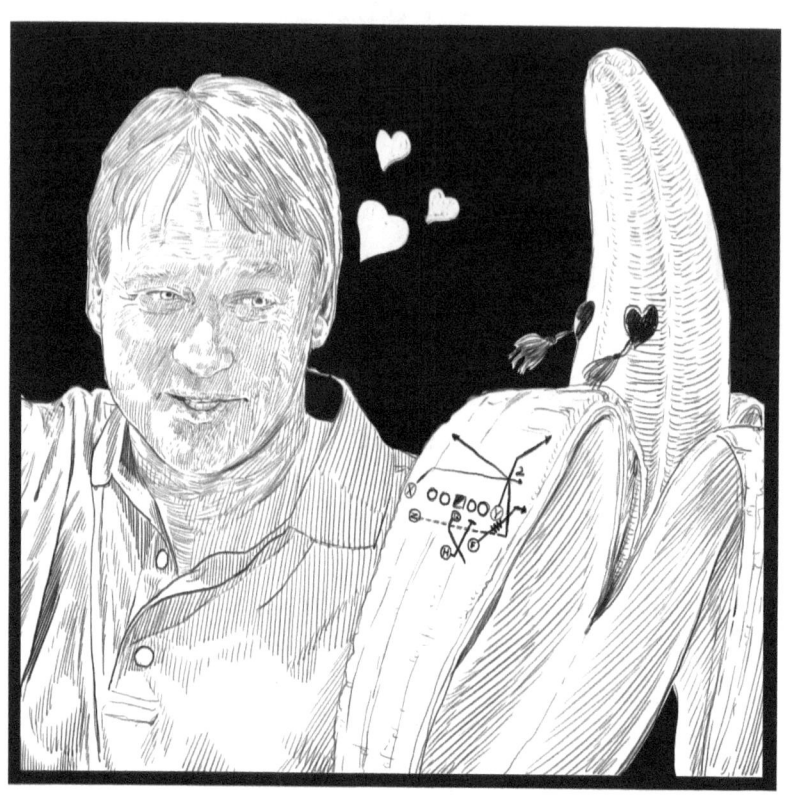

John Gruden

Do you love football?
Do you talk to bananas
And they tell you what to call
on third down and six?

Man, I've talked to bananas since the first grade.
There's a Primal Connection
Between a Man and a Banana.
Just like there is with football.

It's our in DNA to love football,
The monkeys played in the jungle
Using poop and fish bones for a pigskin.
Those monkeys, man, they played Raider football.

Man, I love football as much as Mama Gruden.
I hope when I die they cut my body up
And turn me in to seven footballs
That are used in the Super Bowl.

I'll be watching the game in heaven
Having a banana float with monkey gods
Calling the game on cloud made of
Hooter's Hot Wings and Super Bowl rings.

James Harrison

I tried my hand at writing
Political erotica, because
The NFL is turning into
a League for pussies
and someone needed
to take an artistic stand.

Well mother fuckers,
I proud to say
*My Participation Trophy
Turned Me Gay*
is now up on kindle.

I dedicated it to the Steelers,
Rodger Godell,
and you mother fuckers
who always @ me on Twitter.

Hulk Hogan

Listen Brother,
I'm wifeless, titleless,
And I think I got tendentious
But no worries Hulkamaniacs
Cause the sun shines down
On champions & so does
Lady Justice, as we tag team
Gawker and kill them
With our bare words
And drink their blood
with Peter Thiel

Allen Iversion

Weak bitches
Eat
Twizlers
At Practice
Lying
Kings
Indian
N'omads
Buttonomics
Overrated
U-turns
Trounce
Practice,
Rat
Asses
Claiming
Tissue paper
ISIS
Cucks
End of times

OJ

I did it

Lebron James

(featuring William Shakespeare)

Lebron, how do I love thee? Let me count the ways.
I love thee to the depth and breadth and height
My soul can reach, when feeling out of sight
For the ends of being and ideal grace.
I love thee to the level of every day's
Most quiet need, by #TeamHeat and candle-light.
I love thee freely, as men strive for right.
I love thee purely, as they turn from praise.
I love thee with the passion put to use
In my old griefs, and with my childhood's faith.
I love thee with a love I seemed to lose
With my lost saints. I love thee with the breath,
Smiles, tears, of all my life; and, if Sir Riley choose,
Come back to the Miami and be the best.

Michael Jordan

When Miley Cyrus was barely legal
She asked me why I stick my tongue out
When I dunk?

I told that crazy white girl
That I liked to picture licking vaginas
When taking it to the hole.

I said she needs to find her
Vaginal power and harness it,
Causes it's all in the tongue,
And in the pussy lips—
That is where greatness lies
And motivates you to be great.

I told her no-ass that when you're so great
You can be black and have a Hitler mustache
And people will still buy underwear from you.

She asked me what the hardest thing I did
On my road to greatness.

I told that girl it was being involved
In the Disney Film

Space Jam.

I'm still pissed at those Disney Bastards
For putting me in that piece of shit.

But I told that Miley, she could avenge me—

That when she turns legal
She just needs to stick her tongue out
At that little bitch Mickey Mouse
And twerk on the mother fucker's face.

Cause I'm sick of crying,
And I'm on a mission
To make Disney now shed the tears.

Mel Kipper Jr.

This poetry isn't even worth
a 7th round pick.
Where is the speed?
Where are the tight stanza breaks?
This kid Christoph, was ok in college,
but in the big boy book world,
he doesn't have the stuff.
Now, that Billy Collins,
he can write some poetry.
Christoph Paul, he's just a
Instagram-bro Ryan Tannehill.

Ryan Leaf

In my crystal meth days,
I ended up watching porn
For 83 hours straight
And I heard a guy tell
A barely teen girl with braces,
"I'm going to Ryan Leaf
all over your face."
That was my bottom,
So I sobered up
With a purpose
To tell the kids—
Do opiates instead.

Marvin Lewis

You have felonies,
major character issues—
welcome to the team!

Ray Lewis

I danced the devil away.
I am forgiven.
I give such an inspiring speech
that I could sell knives
on QVC
and y'all would buy 12—
the number of Christ's disciples.
Redemption.
It's a song!
It's a dance!
It's a great lawyer!
It's sack on the quarterback
And running in that fumble for a touchdown.
Through Redemption all is possible
Through second chances
I am reborn.

L.T.

This new NFL is as soft as
The strawberry milkshakes
Tom Brady be putting up his ass.

These pussy boys
Eating their avocados
And not smoking crack.

In my day, On Saturday nights
I snorted cocaine off buttholes,
The combination of the butthole smell
And the cocaine gave me that extra edge.

On Sundays I'd be the Angel of Death
Giving concussions and emotionally
Neutering all quarterbacks.

Now this these bitch boys,
Want to play capture the flag
While rubbing their clitorises
And drinking Gatorade mimosas

That's not my football,
That's softball for soy boys.

Marshawn Lynch

I wrote this poem so I won't get fined.
I wrote this poem so I won't get fined.
I wrote this poem so I won't get fined.
I wrote this poem so I won't get fined.
I wrote this poem so I won't get fined.
I wrote this poem so I won't get fined.
I wrote this poem so I won't get fined.
I wrote this poem so I won't get fined.
I wrote this poem so I won't get fined.
I wrote this poem so I won't get fined.
I wrote this poem so I won't get fined.
I wrote this poem so I won't get fined.
I wrote this poem so I won't get fined.
I wrote this poem so I won't get fined.
I wrote this poem so I won't get fined.
I wrote this poem so I won't get fined.
I wrote this poem so I won't get fined.
I wrote this poem so I won't get fined.

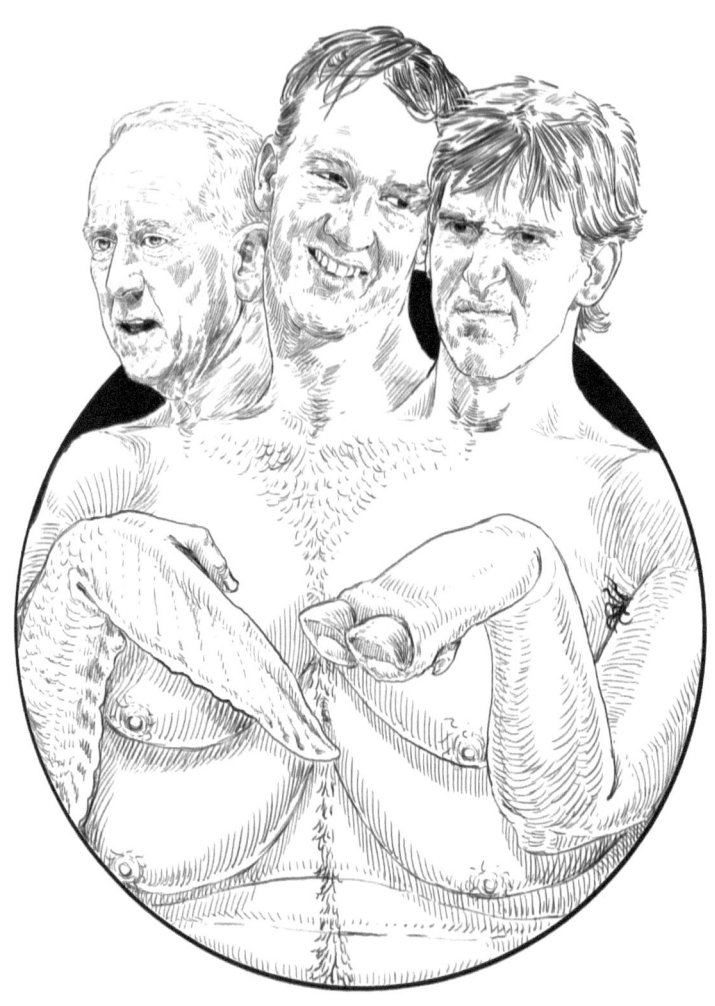

The Mannings

*On the set of a Papa John's Commercial *

Archie: Peyton, this pizza tastes like shit. It's the San Diego Chargers of pizza

Eli: I think it's pretty good.

Archie: Eli you used to eat paste even in your teen years.

Peyton: That wasn't always paste.

Eli: Paste or cum taste better than this shitty pizza.

Peyton: Just eat the pizza and smile for the camera.

Eli: I don't want to

Archie: Eat the pizza Eli and smile for the cameras!

Eli: When can I finally stop eating this pizza, dad?

Archie: If you win won more super bowl you will never have to eat Papa John's again.

Eli: Deal.

Dan Marino

Retirement has been hard
And I still feel restless
About never winning a Super Bowl.

That ring haunts my dreams
And makes me do bad things in real life,
Like send death threats to Don Shula
Because he forgot how to coach
A defense in the eighties.

Some days, I send drones over Tom Brady's house
Just to stare at his Super Bowl rings.

For therapy, I decided to act in
My retirement communities local play.

I'm playing Sméagol in the Lord of The Rings,
And they'll be using Joe Montana's 84 ring
To help me give a great performance.

Please come out and support this play
Or else I will have to act in
Ace Ventura 3: Nature Calls Again.

Floyd Mayweather

Uncle Scrooge is a bitch.
Should have just punched those ghosts out.

If some mothers fucking ghosts tried to take
my money I'd Ghostbust their asses back to hell.

Too many haters, and you can't count on these
bitches, you can only count on your boys.

Me & Trump Jr, are sick of all these thot-cucks
and we are going to Hangover
this mother fucker in Vegas.

I'm a be Bradley Cooper's character,
Trump Jr. gonna be the dentist,
& McGregor can be that weird little guy.

We the new wolf pack and alpha females
better watch out, we gonna tame that ass.

We the wolves of the desert & the world is my ring
and I ain't stopping till someone knocks me the
fuck out.

Vince McMahon

In this shitty poetry book
I'm going to list why the XFL
Is going to succeed this time.

1. We play football made with human brains.
It will make it more primal and with brains Being
pink, we can have breast cancer awareness Every
month so the feminists will be happy.

2. We clone HeHateMe and have 22 of his clones
on the fields for kick offs, and every team
gets HeHateMe clones to play on Special Teams.

3. We don't just stand during the anthem,
we hold our balls for Lady Liberty
and if anyone doesn't, you kick them
right in the dick if they disrespect the flag.

4. No coin flip, arm wrestling. That's right,
Cobra-style arm wrestling for who gets
the ball first. It gets the show rolling.

5. Cheerleaders won't dance
they will only shoot ak-47 after every
sack, first down, and they can pretend
to felate the guns after a touchdown.

Cam Newton

Even though I stole laptops at UF
And slept with lots of hoes before marriage,
My Lord and Savior, Jesus Christ, has
Forgiven me.

When the day comes that I pass,
I know I'm going to straight to heaven,
To the pass the football to Jesus.

I know Jesus loves football
And every Sunday he plays
7 on 7 against his Dad.

Jesus is going to pick me
Every game to be his QB,
Running the read option.

But I won't run, I'll throw touchdowns,
To Jesus, though he'd probably have
Bad hands cause of... you know...
When he died for my sins

Tony Parker

I eat defenses like I do
Mi ma-ma's
Délicieux frog legs.
The center is like snails,
That I crack as I escargot
To the hoop.
I *la meilleur*,
I *manager* all,
Mi *manager* anything
near court,
Even teammate wife's vaginas.
It ok, in France,
We share *amour*.
We don't pass ball
Only pass épouse around,
It ok, normal in Parie,
C'est la vie in San Antonio.

Meta World Peace

I ran into those stands
To start a fight
But I found enlightenment
When I punched
Those fools—
Realizing
I was
Punching
My
Self

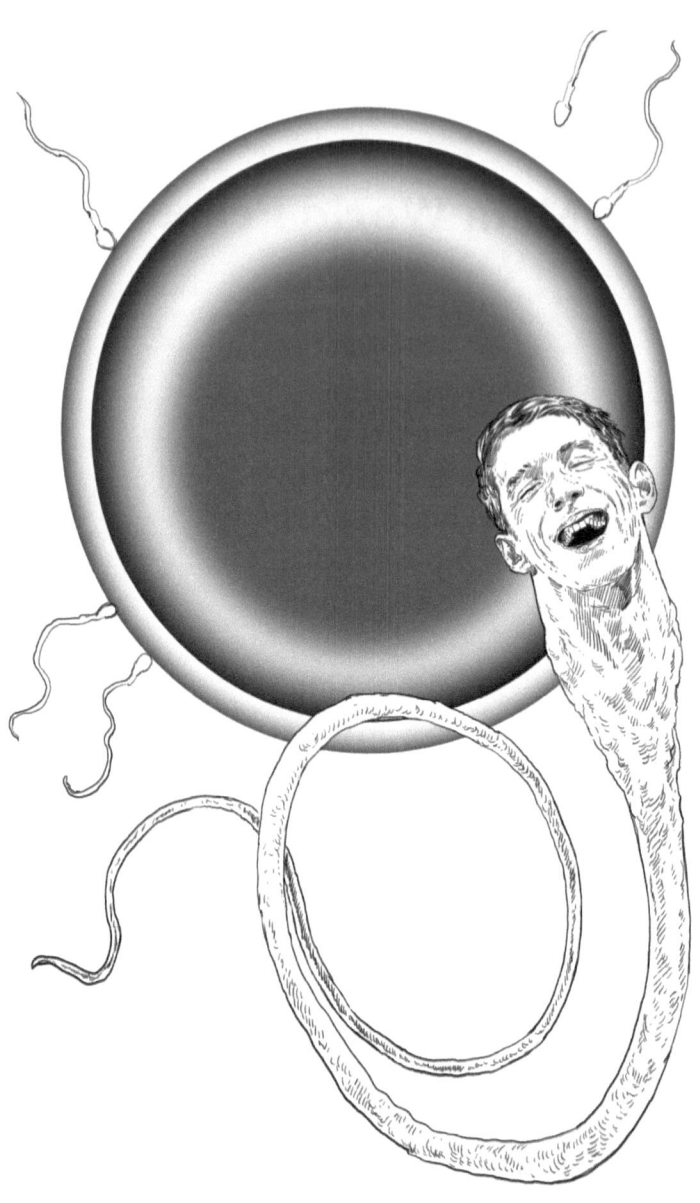

Michael Phelps

When I was training for the gold
I read the evolutionary psychology
book, "Your Inner Fish."

Swimming is the primordial art
of the sperm war.

The pool is the fallopian tubes
and the Olympics are
globalization ovulation.

Gold medals are my peacock feathers
and my monkey ears

are a reminder of our past,
when we swam with fish
and the looks of men were judged

on speed and their inner shark,
for when women
see my back stroke
their inner fish
gets wet.

A-Rod

I miss playing catch with Madonna.

She really learned to ball
On the set of a League of Their Own.

We'd play catch and she'd tell me how
Taylor Swift and Britney
are overrated bitches.

I'd tell her I feel the same way
about Jeter and Langoria.

Then we'd shoot each other up
with steroids
& 69.

Dennis Rodman

Sometimes when Kim and I hang
We just binge Saved by the Bell.
Our favorite episode
Is the Friends Forever one.
Kim says that I'm Zack mixed Lisa Turtle
And he says he is strong like AC Slater,
Attractive as Kelly Kapowksi,
And as intelligent as Screech.
I don't argue with him
Cause I don't want to be fed
To his pet sharks.
The only friends besides me
Kim has
Are his sharks
And President Trump.

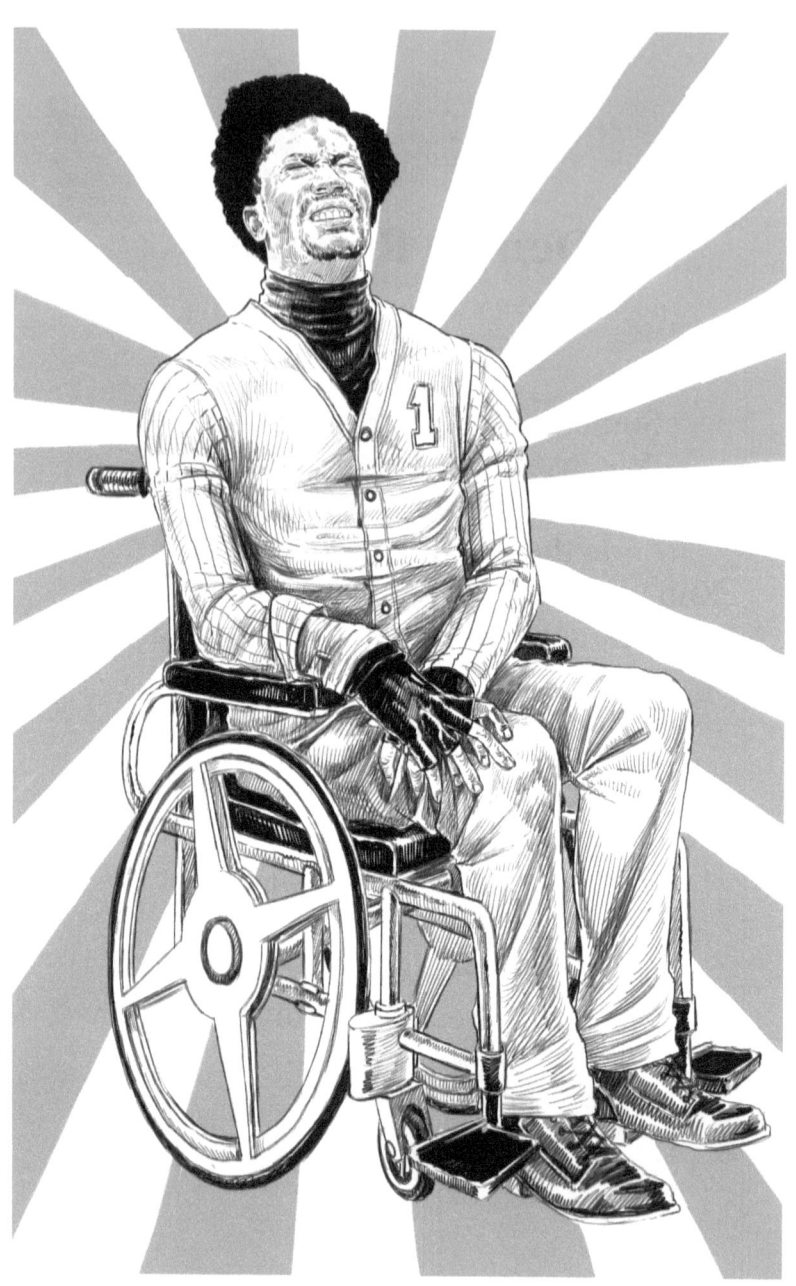

Derrick Rose

NOT MY KNEEE
EEEEEEEEEEE
EEEEEEEEEEE
EEEEEEEEEEE
EEEEEEEEEEE
EEEEEEEEEEE
EEEEEEEEEEE
EEEEEEEEEEE
E!!!!!!!!!!!!!!!!!!!!!!
!!!!!!!!!!!!!!!!!!!!!!!!!

Ben Roethlisberger

Route reads are solid ways to pick up first downs
Antonio is my guy
Passing downfield to him
Is always a way to keep the defense honest
Standard zone reads are tough
Tenacity is key to make it to the end zone

Ronaldo

(Guest Poem by my buddy Jerry)

Ronaldo, oh Ronaldo,
The king of foot ball-o;
That statue of you looks real weird.

Ronaldo, oh Ronaldo,
You sleep with super models,
And don't have a beard.

You'll never win the World Cup,
Everyone says so.
Cry yourself to sleep
On your mountain of pesos.

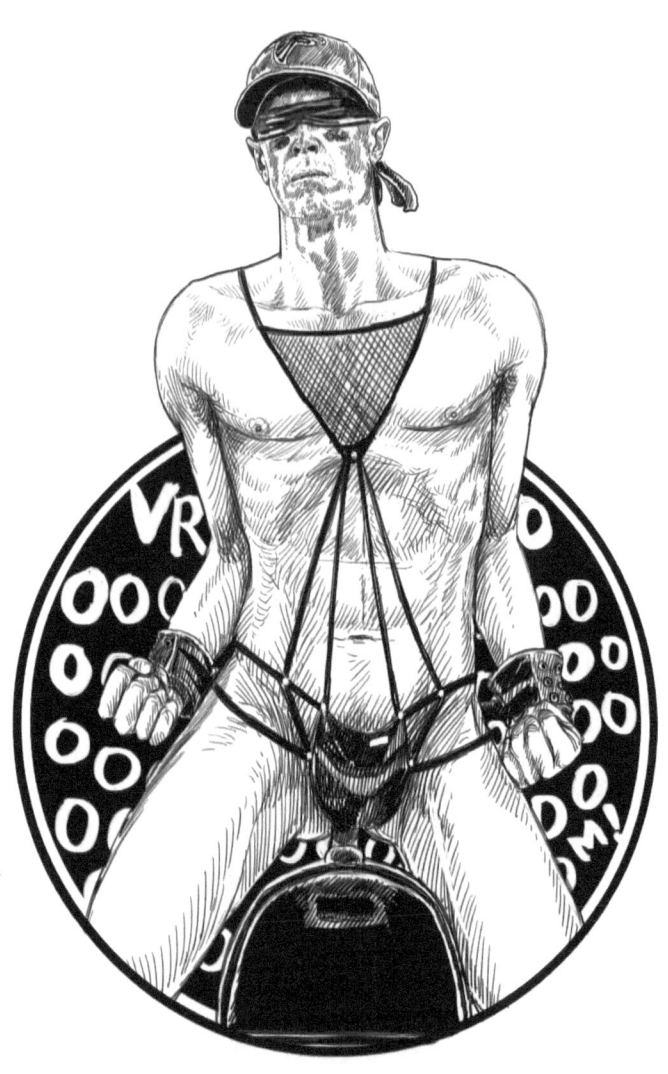

Matt Ryan

To motivate me
I go see a dominatrix,
who lives in the suburbs of Atlanta.

We watch my Super Bowl tape
playing only the 4th quarter
While my master Mrs. Blank

puts cigarettes out on my chest
and pees on the burn to ease the pain—
then she makes ride a Sybian.

It still doesn't hurt
or humiliate as me
as much as that Super Bowl loss.

Nick Saban

The Devil Went Down to Alabama
Looking for champions to steal,
He was in a bind,
Cause Daunte Culpeeper's knee died,
And the Dolphins were going to scratch his deal.
When he came across a special town
That Billy Bryant found,
And said, "Boy, let me tell you what:
The NFL is really tough,
But you gotta follow your gut
And if you care to take a dare,
I'll bring you gold fair and square.
Boy, but give the Devil his due,
He bet a fiddle of gold he take SEC
And told those southern boys,
"I'm better than you."
Little boys laughed
and the Big Ten fiddled around,
But every year the Devil
believes he'll get the crown.

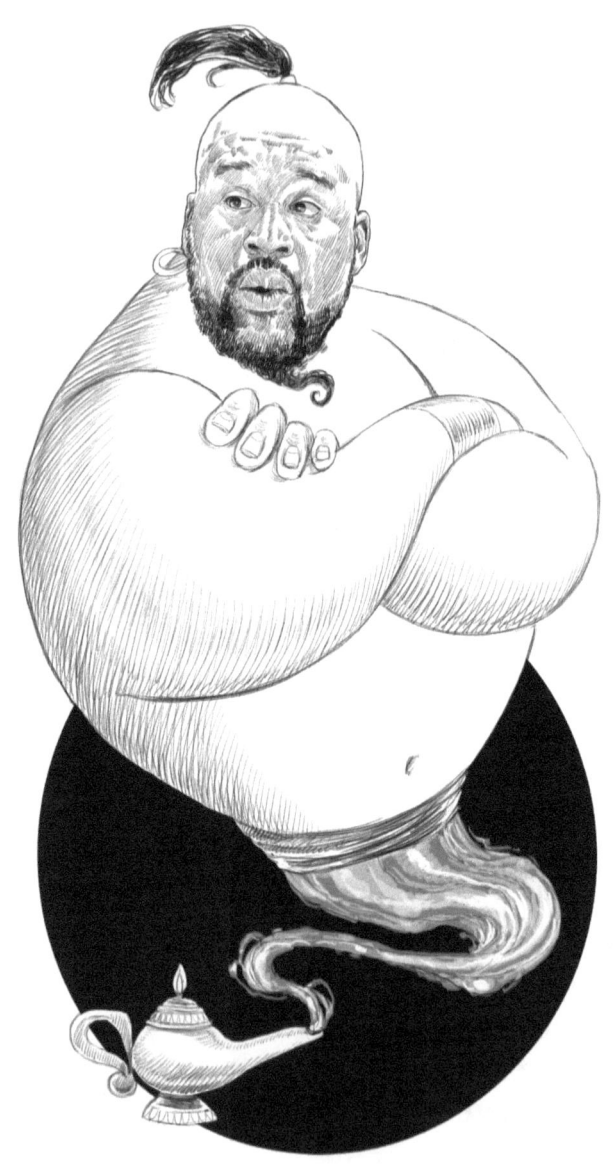

Shaq

I once had dinner
with Nelson Mandela
at The Sizzler.
I talked to him
about doing
a rap opera
about his life,
but he said
that was a
stupid idea
& I should
just focus
on my free throws.
So the great Aristotle,
became a genie in a bottle
but Sinbad stole my spot,
and the space time continuum,
and now, I still eat at The Sizzler
wondering if Shazam is really me,
or am I Kazam & did Nelson Mandela
die or was it Morgan Freeman's career?

Maria Sharapova

Every time I make score
I give thanks to Putin.
He make me so proud
To be Russian Tennis Superstar.
He reading this book right now,
Putin, read all books.
Putin everywhere, HELP ME,
Win championship for him
HE GOING TO KILL MEsopotamia
If they challenge us.
Tennis great, and I AM SCARED
To one day not be able to play
Please SEE I A, good girl who will
SAVE ME, A game with a good serve.

Skip vs Stephen A.

I'm an athlete of words.

I eat chicken broccoli and fart during
The commercials,
To get into Stephen A Smith's head.

It's in my contract that I can fart
During commercial

Stephen held his nose
And said, "It's either me or Skipp

Like Lebron
He couldn't handle 'fart' defense.

***

SO DISRESPECTFUL!
DIS
RE
SPECT
FUL!

Skip has no gamesmanship
Skip has no respect.

***

It wasn't disrespectful
It was smart debate
My clutch genes
Can make me fart on demand.

***

I demanded that fool get fired,
But not a day goes by
Where I don't miss that
Lebron hating mother fucker.

Ndamukong Suh

I stomped on Tom Brady's balls.
He liked it.
It made him feel less
Guilty
About Deflategate.
Quarterbacks man,
It's all psychological
For them.

So now that fool calls me
When he's eating his
Avocado ice cream.
Wanting me
To stomp his balls.

His trainer pays me
Under the table
And Giselle is cool with it,
Her and I are now friends
And do pilates together.

Tim Tebow

I'm not
going to
tell you
what to do
or who to worship,
I am just going to tell you
that life is about possibilities
& dreams, and poetry is what you do.
Poetry is about disregarding logic, statistics,
& building up a romantic truth & making it real.
You can read this book & laugh & take away nothing,
or you can go look in the mirror and ask yourself
who do you want to be? What do you want to do?
You can see the odds, but through the power
of belief you can divide them into what
will make you succeed. You are you
and you can become who you are,
...and that will be true poetry...

Manti Te'o

My girlfriend would write me poems
on my MySpace page.

My girlfriend is like so cool.

I'm trying to go on double date
with Drew Brees,

but he shakes his head no
every time I ask him

to meet my girlfriend.

Drew is so disciplined
just like my girlfriend.

Dick Vitale

WHAT'S UP BABY
I'M DONE WITH BASKETBALL
AND I'M DOING SLAM POETRY, BABY,
I'M GOING FULL TIME TO OPEN MICS
BABY, SHOWING THESE YOUNGSTERS
& HUSTLERS THAT I'M THE
VILLANOVA OF THIS NEW VAUDVILEE
SCENE BABY, UNCLE DICKIE OWNING
THE CITY OWNING THE MIC, GET TENS
EVERY NIGHT, INVITING FRIENDS
ON FACEBOOK
TO COME TO MY SHOW, BABY,
BUT THEY DON'T COME, BABY,
THEY NEVER COME,
BUT MY WIFE DOES
OH YEAH BABY
TRIPLLE DOUBLE
WORD PLAY, BABY,
I'M THE BEST, BABY,
THE ONE & ONLY
DICKIE V. BABY

JJ Watt

Did you know I was the first non-pimp
invited to the Playa's Ball Convention?

Pimps literally kept their 'hoes in line'
By saying, "Don't make me JJ Watt your ass."

I think hitting women is wrong
And prostitution is immoral—
I try to be woke y'all,
but I don't want use my white male privilege
to look down on Pimp Culture.

                Game
              Recognize
                Game.

Russel Westbrook

Sometimes I get so bored in Oklahoma
That I put on my favorite Tommy Hilfiger outfit
And start fires in my back yard.

I like to watch it burn,
Till the fire starts talking to me

They tell me things thing I already know,
Like that point guards that pass are bitches.

And the apocalypse will happen before 2050,
But we will be in Mars and the flames
Will keep the Neo-Xenuians away.

I am not just a point guard anymore,
I am the prophet of Oklahoma
And I will continue to be one
Unless they trade me back to L.A.

Please, please, please,
Save me from the flames!
Send me back to L.A.

Ricky Williams

I once tried to smoke
Dave Wannstedt's mustache.
It didn't get me high
But I could taste
Mediocrity
And didn't like it.
But when I did Yoga
With white girls in Europe
I learned that duality
And definitions
Are just ego
Running to no end zone.

Serena Williams

There was supposed to be
A 30to30 ESPN Special on me
From Ratchet to Racquet:
The Serena Williams Story.

I am almost gave it the green
Light because these hoes on the
Court know I'm still ghetto.

I'll shove a ball down your throat
If get you shit wrong.

This ain't volleyball bitches.

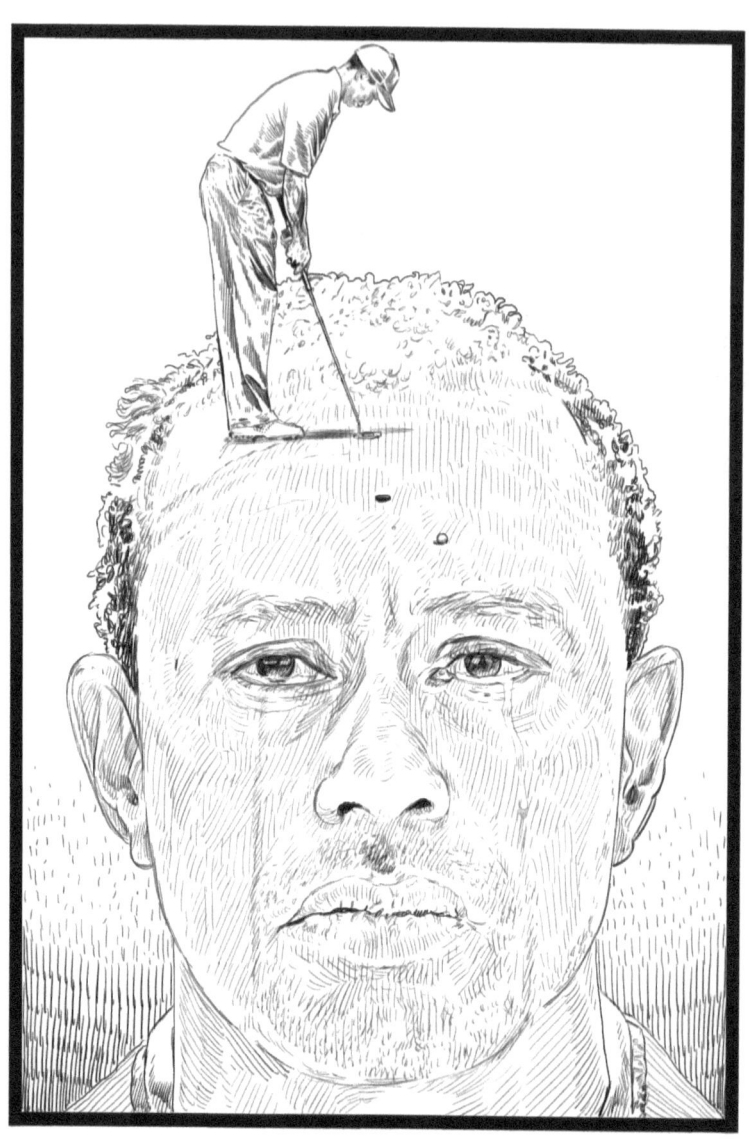

Tiger Woods

When I was seventeen
My dad and I travelled to the Himalayas
To get my golf clubs
Blessed by the monks

We travelled far living off
Snow and goat milk.
It was miserable
But I was happy to bond with my father.

When we reached the top
Our goat milk and snow
Turned into ice cream,
Which we gave to the monks as a gift.

The monks blessed it and said,
"Your power will be absorbing
Beautiful yin energy and giving
Ice cream to your beloved."

The monks left my father and I.
We walked down unsure
What they meant and father

Was pissed that they didn't bless my clubs.

We got back to practicing
But my swing only got worst
And even my short game dropped.
I felt cursed by those monks.

I drove back from practice
And stopped to get some ice cream at Perkins,
Hoping to feel some magic
That I felt with my father in the mountains.

And there was magic,
I saw my favorite porn star
Jenna Jameson's titties popping out
While she was eating pancakes.

I moved my eyes up to hers
And she gave me a look
That she could see my greatness,
So I followed her to her car,

And I fucked her doggystyle while
She ate a Fudge Brownie Supreme
And the day with the monks came to me,
I could see future golf shots I'd make.

I could see the trophies, but I knew
For me to keep the coming
I'd have to find more porn stars
And fuck them behind Perkins.

WNBA

The only thing men hate
more than us
is poetry.
Good luck selling
this stupid ass book.

Jay-Z

Yo, I'll manage your sports career
If you join Tidal,
And get paid in Lemonade.

GAME OVER
BUT THERE ARE

BONUS DRAWINGS!

BIOS OF
THE POET
&
THE ARTIST

Christoph Paul is an awarding-winning humor author and a suffering Miami Dolphin fan, but a happy fan & alum of the 2017 National Champions UCF Knights. He talks about sports on Twitter & YouTube and plays in the band Dionysus Effect.

Jim Agpalza is an illustrator from 50th state. He now resides outside of Portland, Oregon with his wife, two kids, and cat and ghost cat. He once purchased a small baggie from a homeless man which turned out to be chewed up yellow pages. Whop wah.

ALSO BY CLASH BOOKS

HORROR FILM POEMS
by Christoph Paul & Joel Amat Güell

GIRL LIKE A BOMB
by Autumn Christian

TRAGEDY QUEENS: STORIES INSPIRED BY LANA DEL REY & SYLVIA PLATH
edited by Leza Cantoral

DARK MOONS RISING IN A STARLESS NIGHT
Mame Bougouma Diene

NOHO GLOAMING & THE CURIOUS CODA OF ANTHONY SANTOS
Daniel Knauf (Creator of HBO's Carnivàle)

IF YOU DIED TOMORROW I WOULD EAT YOUR CORPSE
Wrath James White

THE ANARCHIST KOSHER COOKBOOK
Maxwell Bauman

NIGHTMARES IN ESCTASY
Brendan Vidito

THE VERY INEFFECTIVE HAUNTED HOUSE
Jeff Burk

CLASH

WE PUT THE LIT IN LITERARY

CLASHBOOKS.COM

Twitter, IG, FB @clashbooks

www.ingramcontent.com/pod-product-compliance
Lightning Source LLC
Chambersburg PA
CBHW030115100526
44591CB00009B/407